sunil gawde

essays

ranjit hoskote
jitish kallat

foundation b & g

Special thanks:

To my family, for being there
always: Pappa, Usha, Durga.

Shri Mohan Dada - Parivar for being
my strength, especially Madan.

Harsha Bhatkal
Ranjit Hoskote
Jitish Kallat

Sakshi Gallery
Sucheta & Anantha Kamat
Chandrakant Patel
Meenal & Rajesh Kapadia
Suruchi & Ashish Choksi

Photo credits:
Sachin Powle, Shankar Natarajan,
Sunil Gawde, Vinay Mahidhar, Som
Subro Sarkar, Amit Bhandare,
Madhu Kapparath, Nirmal Jain

All my assistants and my technical
team for being deeply involved with
my ideas

www.sunilgawde.com

Cover: *Still Alive – II* (detail)

(4282)
ISBN : 978-81-7991-534-9

First published 2009

Published by
Ramdas Bhatkal for
Popular Prakashan Pvt. Ltd.
301, Mahalaxmi Chambers
22, Bhulabhai Desai Road
Mumbai 400 026
India

Printed in India by
Ajanta Offset & Packaging Ltd. New
Delhi - 110002

This book is dedicated to my mother, Mai,
who introduced me, in her loving and unassuming way,
to the wonders of the universe.

sunil gawde

Contents

Preface

I was at the Sakshi Gallery in Mumbai in early November 2008 and had just finished viewing one of Sunil Gawde's sculptures from his "Bulb" series, when news arrived that Sunil had just been invited to participate in the 53rd Venice Biennale. There was much jubilation all around and congratulations were certainly in order. Sunil himself, in his typical understated style, was muted in his response, perhaps anxious about the months of toil ahead. And now, with his work for the Biennale, "Alliteration" on the high seas on its way to Venice, there is a feeling of relief and perhaps anticipation.

We at Foundation B&G felt it would be an appropriate time to publish a book that would be a mid-career review of Sunil Gawde, the sculptor. One that would trace his work over the past two decades as he transitioned from being an abstract painter to one of the important and innovative sculptors in contemporary Indian art. Apart from being a tribute to Sunil's participation in the Venice Biennale, we felt this book would be in keeping with Foundation B&G's continuing endeavour to develop a serious knowledge infrastructure for India's contemporary visual arts. The Foundation has planned a publishing programme that includes entry-level, intermediate and specialist books.

We are delighted that Ranjit Hoskote, transnational art critic, cultural theorist and curator, agreed to edit this book and contribute an essay to it. Ranjit has followed Sunil's career closely over two decades. In his essay, he traces Sunil's shift from a solitary painterly practice to a richly collaborative and expansive practice as sculptor and installation artist. He identifies the dialectic of reason and sensory experience as pivotal to Sunil's work, and locates Sunil's metaphysics in the context of post-industrial Mumbai.

We are also thankful to Jitish Kallat, himself an internationally acclaimed artist who also writes on art, for contributing a reflection on Sunil's work for the Venice Biennale. Titled 'A Moonologue with Sunil Gawde's Alliteration', Jitish's essay presents a fellow artist's perspective on the making and potential artistic contexts of Sunil's Venice work, suggesting several trajectories from which one may approach his evolving artistic concerns.

Harsha Bhatkal
Publisher, Foundation B&G
May 2009

Instrumental Variations:
Reflections on Sunil Gawde's Sculptural Works

Ranjit Hoskote

I. A Passage to Sculpture

'Alliteration', Sunil Gawde's large-scale kinetic sculptural work for the 53rd Venice Biennale 2009, distils a decade of intense engagement with what it means for a painter to produce sculpture in the terrain between game and scientific instrument, between interiority and the public domain. In the process, he has re-investigated the formal questions of gravity and lightness that have exercised generations of sculptors before him. He has asked himself whether the sculptural artefact ought to be introverted and maintain a silent distance from the viewer, inviting gradual attention; or whether it should turn outwards, purposefully and sociably, to activate a viewership around itself? During the last few years, Gawde has calibrated his works along various scales; he has positioned them at different points of intensity between the austere and the ludic, aura and kitsch, artisanal density of texture and conceptual clarity of image.

Gawde first received acclaim in India, in the early 1990s, for his practice of an abstraction that combined the powerful sweep of gesture with a minute calibration of effects. [1] In the years that followed, through periods of intense work and reflection in India and Scotland, he refined this approach through a series of balancing acts, negotiating between the sensuality of his material and the elusiveness of what lay just beyond the reach of form; he came to be recognised as a strong claimant to the mantle of the established abstractionist styles. [2]

The success of a style, however, can be a curse disguised as a blessing. Unlike many artists presented with a similar double edge, Gawde saw through the seductions of acclaim. Towards the end of the 1990s, he went through a creative dissatisfaction: a restlessness, articulated tentatively at first and then more consistently, began to vein his practice. It seemed to him that, accomplished as it was, his idiom of gestural abstraction had become self-enclosed, fixed in its twin emphases on the act of painting as choreographic performance and the product of that act as a thickly layered, densely textured surface generative of *bas relief* motifs thrown up by impasto spatula-work.

By 2000, Gawde renounced the sumptuous textural passages and coloristic exuberance with which his art had been associated: his paintings became minimalist. Soon, he expanded his scope to include more philosophical questions concerning the relationship of art objects to the concentric contexts of exhibition, interpretation and consumption. He became preoccupied with the manner in which art-works are situated, for viewers, in the domains of language and artefactuality: as things named, as special objects among regular objects. His search for such connections between forms and names led him, by degrees, to explore sculpture and the sculpture-installation.

At first, Gawde treated sculpture as a mode through which to study the relationship between object, space and time. His early experiments with the sculptural involved a play of dislocation in which objects were alienated from their normal sites and functions; painted images and readymades were juxtaposed, and prompted to behave in incongruous or idiosyncratic ways relative to the expectations of viewers. Having briefly tested out combinations of objects and phrases based on visual double entendre, the artist launched himself on a trajectory that would generate kinetic sculptures and sculpture-installations of memorable power. Some of these were interactive and loquacious, or otherwise invited a substantial degree of viewer participation; others were relatively self-possessed and classical in their repose. All of these works, however, took Gawde beyond pictorial space and into social space. [3]

Crucially, Gawde's passage from painting to sculpture and installation has involved a seismic shift in his studio practice. As a painter, he was a solo performer, with assistants employed only to clean the heavy-duty cleavers and spatulae that he used, or to move large paintings around and attend to the routines of the workspace. As a sculptor and installation artist, however, he has necessarily had to make the transition to a collaborative workshop practice of the kind that is now widely prevalent internationally. He now works closely with technical specialists adept at understanding the moods and capacities of metal and electricity, engineers who can advise the artist on material stress and structural factors, and mission-specific crews of casters, carpenters, welders and other skilled artisans. This builds into a mutually enriching process of dialogue and discovery.

II. Light Objects, Metal Shadows and Subtle Moves

In April 2005, Gawde presented an exhibition of kinetic sculptures and sculpture-installations, titled 'Blind Bulb etc.' The suite of eight objects that constituted this exhibition marked a breakthrough in his art: they occupied the mid-ground between formal sculpture on the one hand, and the fairground or science-exhibition working model on the other. Some of them were mechanical devices, menacing toys, operated by simple motor and gear operations. Others were collapsible sculptures, propelled by means of springs, guy-ropes or belt drives. In each case, though, the primary engine of the art-work was conception.

The works that Gawde presented in 2005 came accompanied by a whiff of Poe: they spoke of time and extinction, the fragility of our human hours, of duration, and the ease with which life can be snuffed out. From 'Blind Bulb etc.' onwards, also, Gawde's palette and textures became almost monastically austere. Now, his preferred surfaces are transparent fibreglass, dead-matte black, brown and flesh-coloured rubber-coated lycra, and steel that is either left dull or polished to mirror grade.

In 'Blind Bulb etc.', the artist explored the world of the sleeping object that awakes to the viewer's touch and gaze: the metal butterfly that is triggered off by our moment of looking; the spring that works its way around the pendulum bob, dragging and raising itself by sheer will power; the gigantic bulb that, sheathed in black, refuses to answer us; or its twin, which looks back at us with a quizzical glass eye; and the shoal of moons that dip in and out of view on a darkened sky map, pursuing their relentless logic of rotation, revolution and eclipse, marking off our circles and ellipses, our hours and days.

The mise-en-scene of this exhibition emphasised the mandate of attentiveness to the smallest and most imperceptible movements – which are the most vital and crucial intervals of passage, since the act of recording them attests to the artist's vigilance to change. This interest in minute calibration has long played a special role in Gawde's process (it was memorialised, for instance, in the title of his 2001 show, '1 mm'). [4] In the background to these meditations lurks that eminence grise of much that is cryptic and quixotic, resistant and interrogative in contemporary art: Duchamp, with his celebrated insistence on the fractional and infinitesimal, the amount of dust that settles on a page in a second, the pressure of air against glass in a still room. For Gawde, his art is now an orchestral performance, the music made by light objects, metal shadows and subtle moves. [5]

Gawde's butterfly, perched on an I-beam, is ambidextrous between self and world: its wings are blade-thick above and silver below, with holes punched or cut out of them like bites. To look at it is to look at yourself and the environment in which you and the object are placed in fortuitous encounter. The holes in its wings are like passages into parallel universes; but sometimes, you look through them and find yourself back in your own world, re-entering via surprise. The butterfly's body is a sword with an ornamental pommel, borrowed from a gaudy present-day Chinese display piece and reshaped. This metal insect's movements are programmed to be deliberately erratic, so that the wings remain frozen for minutes before creaking suddenly into life, surprising the unwary visitor to the studio or gallery. We savour the industrial lyricism of the butterfly's exposed, semi-rusted, sharp-edged surfaces, its smooth but audible gear mechanism. In 2007, Gawde extended this work into an ensemble titled 'Virtually Untouchable – III', presenting three wall-mounted butterflies executed in mirror-finish stainless steel. The circumstances of illumination and shadow were as generative of this work as their punched wings and sword-bodies.

Gawde's giant pendulum image, made in steel polished to serve as a mirror and suspended against a black tower-box, oscillates gently. What seizes our attention is the spring that is programmed to move counter-clockwise along the rim of the pendulum's circular bob, against the conventional motion of time. It gathers itself up into a hump and stretches out, propelling itself forward in a curious movement that is half-leap and half-creep, seemingly abortive but efficacious.

All we see of the device that Gawde refers to as the worm, when we first approach it, is a coiled shiny-brown tube with flesh-toned ends, lying flat along the thin upper surface of a long box that plated with mirrors on all sides. Made from rubber-coated cloth that produces a somewhat garish *faux*-leather effect, this phallic device works on the same principle as the spring on the rim of the pendulum bob, although it is proportionally much larger. It gathers itself up in a hump, but does not move forward as the spring does; rather, it falls back limply, almost sighing as it does. The impression, with the alternate tumescence and flaccidity of the device, is suggestive of a failure of nerve: a metaphor for the predicament of stasis made more tragic by the making of futile motions.

Look, now, at Gawde's troika of bulbs: three abodes of evasive genies, three tombs for the proverbial blind mice, three bodies translated into metaphor? Each of these objects is a giant replica of an electrical light-bulb: the first is made in transparent fibreglass and set at an angle to the viewer. An eyeball, cast in the body of the bulb, looks out at us. The second is coated completely in dead-matte black and suspended from the ceiling by a rope: the light burns within it, invisible to us, symbolic of the introversion of the self-illuminated consciousness in yogic metaphysics. The third is transparent, like the first, but dusted with a coating of carbon powder on the inside. It also boasts a broken, dangling filament that nevertheless moves: this vestigial movement, made possible by a concealed motor, suggests the last residual signs of life in a Voltaic experiment or the stubborn persistence of the will-to-life in a hanged prisoner. Taken together, Gawde's triad of bulbs appears to symbolise three phases of the circuit of life and death, ignorance and enlightenment.

In a more recent installation, 'Fly Away – Swim Closer', Gawde addresses the bulb again: we enter a pitch-dark room to find a giant fibreglass bulb radiating a soft blue glow. Its specially treated surface responds to the ultraviolet light in which the room, unknown and intangible to us, is bathed. Hundreds of metal insects cling magnetically to the surface of the bulb. The sensory experiment of plunging viewers into an environment that they are not biologically equipped to grasp, where they encounter the sense-universe of other species, which respond in radically different ways to light, darkness, security and extinction, produces a refreshing – and humbling – disorientation.

As cryptic and deliciously ambivalent as the giant bulb is Gawde's arrangement of a crescent moon on the floor and the two wings of a butterfly, punched with holes, set at an angle above it. There is a hint, here, of the archetypal figure of Somasekhara: the supreme deity Shiva as Lord of the Crescent Moon, Lord of Time and Eternity, Lord of Nectar and Poison. Between them, the lunar scimitar and the plucked wings carry a total of about 3600 shaving-razor blades set in close-packed rows. There is a piquant, spine-prickling perversity to the superimposition of pleasure and danger, beauty and death, that Gawde explores in this sequence of works.

Gawde has pushed this strategy further in a more recent work, in which he packs hundreds of red, powder-coated razor blades together in the shape of heavy garlands of a kind associated with the ceremonial public culture of South India. To Indians of a certain generation, this image inevitably recalls to mind the assassination, in May 1991, of former Prime Minister Rajiv Gandhi: he had concluded election campaigning and made a brief halt at a small town in Tamil Nadu, where he was killed by a suicide bomber sent out by the Liberation Tigers of Tamil Eelam (LTTE), the insurgent organisation based in northern Sri Lanka. The bomb was concealed in a heavy garland that the assassin placed around Mr Gandhi's neck before she detonated it.

Gawde is fascinated by the differential world pictures that the reason and the senses, respectively, produce. The circumstance of being bodied, sensate selves commits us inescapably to the distortion and interference of our individual faculties and the haptic and representational media we choose to employ. The senses, by themselves, can never guarantee a vision of the world that is accurate, objective and conspectual; such a vision is only made available through models designed by reason. Thus, we are confronted with a central paradox: the senses give us a vivid immediacy of experience but cannot capture the nature of reality; while the operations of the reason are remote from experience but can generate a more accurate portrayal of reality.

This dialectic of experience and reality, sensory surface and conceptual proposition animates a number of Gawde's works, where it is articulated through the metaphor of vision achieved under conditions of distortion. In 'Life', the artist casts a larger-than-life-size germinating seed in bronze; its gleaming surface reflects the world around it, although in wildly distorted curvature: at once a manageably quotidian and a mysteriously cosmic image, the seed draws and stretches us on its skin while denying us entry into its imagined core. In 'Ghost in the Bottle' (2006), a set of mirror-coated glass containers twist, turn and lose shape like a corps of deranged athletes: are they genies in distress; do they bear messages in code; are they wrsetling with repressed desires that will no longer be kept down; or are they symbolic of a signal-receiving self that has begun to deflect the world's anomalies and enigmas in weird, oneiric counter-images? 'Arrival – Departure' is a giant magnifying glass made in steel: a Sufi-like doorless door placed in the middle of the room, it does not magnify but bewilder; anyone who tries to see the world through it is transported into another reality.

'Still Alive' (2008) is a set of four wooden objects carved to resemble heart-shaped balloons. Each is studded with nails and subjected to different levels and intensities of scorching and burning. While the title of this sequence inflects the genre of the still life with irony, the works themselves strongly connote an intertwining of torture, eroticism and the survival of love despite torment and oppression. Although it stages a formal departure from the logic of distorted reflection, 'Still Alive' conveys Gawde's preoccupation with how experience is recorded and inscribed on the receiving subjectivity. [6]

III. Phases of the Moon

Gawde's Venice work, 'Alliteration', was prefigured in a complex 2005 orchestration that he titled '28 moons'. What you saw as you approached this work was a flat, dead-matte black metal wall. In the play of darkness and shadow, you did not notice the 28 circular holes cut out of it, apparently at random. Behind this perforated wall, unseen, were seven belt-driven wheels, their movements choreographing an elaborate dance of the moons. The number 28 stands for the number of days in a lunar month, of course, but the art-work was not bound to any astronomical pattern. Its renditions of waxing, waning, eclipse and full moon were phases of the mind: the wheels, and correspondingly the moons, operated at differential rhythms, invoking different schemata by near-hypnotic means, as brightness arose from and returned to sleep in darkness.

In the same vein, 'Alliteration' (2009) is a complex meditation on the passage of time: a contemplation of the rhythmic flow of waxing and waning, fullness and eclipse, which characterises the life cycle of individuals, empires and universes. 'Alliteration' is, in essence, a large-scale apparatus reminiscent of an orrery, the model of the solar system that many planetariums have on display. The orrery was invented in the early years of the 18th century and intended to demonstrate the positions, phases and relative motions of various celestial bodies. With its combination of beauty and functionality, a distinctive feature of the Scientific Revolution that made the Industrial Revolution possible, the orrery incarnates the classical paradox of science: namely, that science preserves the mystery of the cosmos in the very act of analysing and explaining its workings. Gawde has conceived and presented 'Alliteration' in this spirit of paradox: in it, he offers his viewers both the sorcery of effects and the disclosure of causes.

One side of the work presents a screen-like surface to viewers, a wall on which discs representing moons turn at variable speeds, dipping in and out of view. But the reverse side is open, naked to the eye, without hood or baffle: a candid disclosure of the mechanism of linked sprocket, chain, motor and turning wheels that breathes life and movement into Gawde's 1.5-ton device. For, despite its massiveness and sheer presence, 'Alliteration' is a test run for the elusive, fugitive and ephemeral aspects of our experience as travellers through space and time: aspects that lie just beneath the radar of everyday palpability. It is with some deliberation that I choose the word 'device' to describe this sculpture: it is at once a machine that has designs upon the viewer and the world; a heraldic symbol that makes cryptic allusion to transitions of various denominations; and a tool to assist us in our understanding of how various disciplines, now regarded as separate and distinct, were once conjoined in a common quest for illumination.

Gawde's title, which cross-codes the visual with a device drawn from poetry, refers to the manner in which the multiple moon discs in 'Alliteration' rise and fade away on its surface, their whites showing through at periodic intervals: consonants in a sentence composed of small revelations, they repeat one another, cadences that echo and intensify one another in combinations that remain unpredictable to viewers standing before the sculpture. 'Alliteration' unfolds at several levels simultaneously. It alludes directly to a cosmos calibrated by the interlocking trajectories of suns, moons and planets, but whose workings remain mysterious even when in plain view. It hints, also, at the enigma of personality, whether of the individual or the planet, at mental and climatic states shaped by the metronome of the moon, with its fluctuating rhythm of tidal effects. And perhaps most subtly, with understated eloquence, it reflects on a society that has made the transition from an industrial past to a future in which the machine is a splendid ruin rather than engine of profit, quiescent memorial to fortune rather than turbulent generator of change.

In 2002, the curator and cultural activist Rajeev Sethi invited Gawde to contribute to the constellation of art works and projects that he was in the process of mobilising at the time. Gawde proposed a large mobile installation, inspired equally by his interest in the iconography of the supreme deity Shiva as *Maha-Kala* or Guardian of Eternity, and by his reading of Galileo's revolutionary discovery of the phenomenon of planetary satellites in the solar system. While this particular project did not fructify into final shape, the attendant research and experimentation brought about a definitive alteration in Gawde's artistic course.

Voicing the vivid significance of these experiences, the artist notes that his sense of scale was actively transformed: "The Sanskrit poets tell us that Shiva puts the moon in his hair like a flower. I could not look at the sky in the same way afterwards." [7] And his readings of how time had been calibrated by monks and physicists, siege tacticians and astrologers, drew him into a concatenation of offices and periods: he had, he records, an epiphanic realisation that the self is only a spirit constantly in transition from one set of temporal constraints to another, moving like an incidental punctuation among cycles that embody the reality of evolution, decay, collapse and regeneration.

'Alliteration' could be read, at its deepest level, as the testament of an artist who has lived through the most momentous transformation of his home city. Born in Bombay/ Mumbai in 1960 and trained in fine art at the historic Sir Jamsetjee Jejeebhoy School of Art, Gawde has seen his city pass from gritty industrial splendour, through the silence of its textile mills and the collapse of its commercial dockyards, to a hectic post-industrial phase of growth dominated by the information, entertainment, retail and knowledge sectors. Several strata of amnesia have overlaid the tactile and visual memory of what the city was like when Gawde was growing up, in which context 'Alliteration' incarnates an oblique archaeology of metropolitan life. [8]

By slowing down and electing to move back to a relatively lower technology, Gawde retrieves the industrial Sublime in all its artisanal substantiality, its rust-and-paint immediacy. 'Alliteration' summons back to mind the magic of how things work, how things are seen to work when you lift off a lid or unscrew a casing: such magic no longer enjoys currency in an epoch whose sensibilities are shaped by the instantaneities of digital technology, by morphing wizardry and virtual-reality games.

If his formal insistence on the curves, cutaways and the explosive surprises of architecture aligns him with Serra, Gawde also references an earlier lineage in this work. In restoring the connection between image-making and engineering, he lays claim to the legacy of the pageant-makers and military engineers of the Renaissance, who doubled as sculptors and painters (it is possible, for instance, that the public of Leonardo's time may well have been more familiar with his masque designs, public statuary and siege engines than with his court-sponsored paintings). I would suggest that 'Alliteration' expresses Gawde's intuition that the *monumental*, retrieved from vacuous public symbolism and re-invested with the charge of private obsession, is one of the few legitimate means of approaching the *cosmic* at a time when such a quest excites either irony or scepticism. Standing in the presence of 'Alliteration' – whether in the workshop where it came to birth in the glare of welder's lamps and the hiss of blowtorches, or in a museum space – we are reminded of how many of the world's great scientific instruments are also monumental objects. Think, for instance, of the Jantar Mantar, Mount Palomar and Hubble: platforms where the mystic would be as much at home as the astronomer.

'Alliteration' is more than a sculpture. It is an occasion for the fine-tuning of metaphysical and historical questions, a field of discussion where the artist's impulses and the viewer's may come into interplay. Walking around this as-yet-unidentified object, watching Sunil Gawde guide his team of technicians through rounds of testing, I think of the appropriateness to this moment of Olafur Eliasson's memorable remark to Hans Ulrich Obrist in a December 2005 conversation between them. A remark that is all the more heroic for coming from the experimenter's toughness rather than the certitude of genius, from the hands-on ethos of the versatile workshop rather than the sedate interior of the classical studio: "Right now I'm trying to make an instrument. It's not working yet, but it will at some point." [9]

(Vienna, March 2009 – Bombay/ Mumbai, April 2009)

Notes & References

1. See Ranjit Hoskote, 'Three Diary Entries: Framing Sunil Gawde over Thirty-six Months' (catalogue essay; Chitrakoot Art Gallery, Calcutta, & Cymroza Art Gallery, Bombay/ Mumbai: February 1994).

2. See Ranjit Hoskote, 'Radium Grass: Sunil Gawde, Paintings 1995-1997' and Clare Henry, untitled essay (catalogue essays; The Mackintosh Museum-Glasgow School of Art, Glasgow: July-August 1997).

3. See unsigned catalogue text for 'Oblique' (Jehangir Art Gallery, Bombay/ Mumbai; Apparao Galleries and Lalit Kala Akademi, Chennai; Faculty of Fine Arts, Baroda; Rabindra Bhavan, New Delhi: between August and December 1998).

4. Ranjit Hoskote, 'The Dynamising Gesture: Recent Works by Sunil Gawde' (catalogue essay for '1 mm'; Sakshi Gallery, Bombay/ Mumbai: September-October 2001).

5. Ranjit Hoskote, 'Eight Moves: Reflections on Sunil Gawde's 'Blind Bulb etc.' ' (Bombay/ Mumbai: Sakshi Gallery, April 2005).

6. A complete visual record of Sunil Gawde's sculptural work may be accessed at www.sunilgawde.com

7. Sunil Gawde, in conversation with Ranjit Hoskote, Bombay: 24 February 2009.

8. For an account of this transformation in Bombay/ Mumbai, and its effects on the political and cultural identity of the metropolis, see Ranjit Hoskote, 'Versions of a Postcolonial Metropolis: Competing Discourses on Bombay's Image', in Klaus Segbers, Simon Raiser and Krister Volkmann eds., *The Making of Global City Regions: Johannesburg, Mumbai/ Bombay, São Paulo, and Shanghai* (Baltimore: The Johns Hopkins University Press, 2007), pp. 258-278.

9. Hans Ulrich Obrist & Olafur Eliasson, *Olafur Eliasson* / The Conversations Series No: 13 (Köln: Walther König, 2008), p. 90.

RANJIT HOSKOTE (born Mumbai, 1969) is a cultural theorist, curator and poet. He is the author of 15 books. These include five collections of poetry, most recently *Vanishing Acts: New & Selected Poems 1985-2005* (Delhi: Penguin, 2006) and *Die Ankunft der Vögel* (München: Carl Hanser Verlag, 2006). He has also written six monographs on artists, most recently *The Crafting of Reality: Sudhir Patwardhan, Drawings* (Mumbai: The Guild, 2008). Hoskote has authored, with the German writer Ilija Trojanow, a history of cultural confluence, *Kampfabsage* (München: Random House/ Blessing Verlag, 2007). Hoskote has collaborated with Atul Dodiya on an artist book, *Pale Ancestors* (Mumbai: Bodhi Art, 2008).

Hoskote was co-curator of the 7th Gwangju Biennale (2008), with Okwui Enwezor and Hyunjin Kim. Since 1994, he has curated 17 exhibitions of modern and contemporary art, including a mid-career retrospective of Atul Dodiya (Japan Foundation, Tokyo, 2001), a lifetime retrospective of Jehangir Sabavala (National Gallery of Modern Art, Delhi and Mumbai, 2005-2006), and a survey exhibition, 'Aparanta: The Confluence of Contemporary Art in Goa' (Escola Medica Cirurgica de Goa, Panjim, 2007).

Hoskote was Fellow of the International Writing Program at the University of Iowa (1995) and writer-in-residence at Villa Waldberta, München (2003). He lives and works in Mumbai.

A MOONOLOGUE WITH SUNIL GAWDE'S 'ALLITERATION'

Jitish Kallat

Sunil Gawde's new work 'Alliteration' is an advanced variation of a similar piece from his key sculptural series titled 'Blind Bulb etc.' (2005). I have a distinct memory of standing before it even as the interplaying black-and-white lunar forms moved at different speeds evoking a mechanical montage of an anomalous sky. In the piece I'd seen earlier, the sky seemed to have somehow gone malignant with moons of differing dimensions metastasized all over; each one was seen waxing and waning at a varying pace as if their individual rotational speeds were in allochronic disarray. This uncanny vision seemed slightly catastrophic as the earth's nearest satellite replaced all the distant stars; and all familiar constellations seemed to have paranormally gone missing from this celestial coordinate system conjured by Sunil Gawde.

We decide to meet at his workshop in Mumbai where 'Alliteration' is being fabricated.

The Playful Transliteration

We meet at a grungy industrial complex in North Mumbai where various kinds of metal fabrications are in process. In one glance the tenor of Gawde's workshop is no different from the activities in the neighbouring factories; however, what sets this enterprise apart is the fact that hard industrial labour and skills are being employed with the poetic and playful intention of making a pigment coated metallic sky. Steel bars are cut into precise right angles; sheave and pulley mechanisms are being tested to meet the strict calculations of the CAD drafting; and noisy momentum tests are being conducted to ensure that the perfunctory backstage circuitry gets programmed to efficiently run this all-steel supernal composition.

To have a quiet and undisturbed conversation on the subterranean objective of this mechanical object we head to a nearby peaceful café. Coincidentally the beginnings of this piece happened half a decade ago when Gawde was invited to consider an unusual artistic commission in this very neighbourhood. He was urged to think of the imagery surrounding the Hindu deity Shiva as a starting point for his piece. This project was peculiar since it is rare to see commissions of this nature in the contemporary Indian art scene that seeks to directly reference religious iconography. Religion was never an explicit theme in Gawde's work during his 28 years of art-making. While he decided to address this commission in an indirect manner, at a personal level he continued to pursue the vast set of images that he had thought of during his short deliberations on the image of the deity.

There are numerous attributes that become a repository of symbols surrounding Lord Shiva: for instance, the tiger-skin attire suggests his attainment as an ascetic, the hourglass shaped drum reveals the rhythmic reverberations of cosmic time, the blue throat is suggestive of the poison he churned and swallowed from the world oceans, and the serpent-garland he wears around his neck cools his poisoned throat. Of these, Gawde was drawn to the miniature crescent moon that Lord Shiva wears in his matted hair. In the Hindu trilogy, Brahma is the creator, Vishnu is the maintainer and Shiva is the destroyer or transformer; the waxing and waning of the moon symbolizes time-cycles but wearing a permanently crescent moon as an ornament makes him an eternal reality beyond cycles of time.

'Alliteration' in a curious way emerged out of a playful transliteration of these religious symbols to take the form of a free-standing art object, a twisted cosmogram, a mechanical toy or a sacred chronometer that concurrently registers the passage of time in several parallel worlds.

The Moonologue

While viewing Sunil Gawde's work-in-progress, two artists from very diverse cultural backgrounds and generations came to my mind; Nam June Paik (b. 1932) and Darren Almond (b. 1971). While their widely differing practices have very little formal or mediumistic affinity with Gawde, a fleeting note on particular works by these artists might aid the viewing of 'Alliteration'.

I thought of Nam June Paik's seminal video 'Moon is the Oldest TV' (1965) where a lunar cycle is created by a magnetic intervention in the television's cathode ray tube, transforming the incoming televised signal into full, gibbous and crescent moons. Another interesting piece is Paik's collaboration with the influential filmmaker Jud Yalkut on the video 'Electronic Moon No. 2' (1969) revealing a deep artistic fascination with the earth's oldest means of nocturnal illumination. In 'Electronic Moon No. 2' the moon is seen as a glowing and shape-shifting mass of mystery as it gets reflected in the waters and finally ends with an interesting eclipse created by the shadow of a male face and a female breast; the mysterious pitch of this video led David Bienstock, erstwhile film curator of The Whitney Museum of American Art, to refer to this work as a modern day film-haiku.

The fact that Gawde wasn't familiar with Paik's and Yalkut's pioneering effort makes it even more interesting when one looks at a short poem he wrote in 2003. I quote: "In the arithmetic of life, The mystery of shadows puzzles me the most. Shadows on the moon, Shadows on the human heart, Always ascending and descending the mystery of soundless shadows, Make me rearrange my beliefs. Because at times I can recognise my own shadow - On the moon. It's God's divine shadow play".

It is fascinating to look at 'Alliteration' alongside Darren Almond's monumental flip-clocks. One of the captivating elements of Almond's mammoth time-machines is the alarming flip of the numeric flap, as if the passage of time itself has a component of threat inscribed in it. The exposed machines at the rear help register the passing moments; while the attached speakers amplify this process to announce the movement of time acoustically, etching an element of fear and unease into its course. The word clock comes from the Celtic root-words *clagan* and *clocca* meaning 'bell', where intervals of time are marked with a set of chimes or a gong; using sound at intervals to record units of time.

The Cyclic Clockwork

In an interesting contrast to Almond's amplified sounding of time, Gawde's 'Alliteration' continues with the gradual, relentless and unchanging hum of the machine at the back. The consistent rotation of the multiple moons evokes time but simultaneously provokes us to ponder on the notions of periodicity and duration. When undivided, time becomes a seamless, intangible stream. Time has no concrete beginning or end until we begin to domesticate it within markers and pollute it with numbers, creating units and fractions that provide us a sense of duration. Left alone without a sense of frequency, time is an endless journey without stations where the only definite reality is the present.

Quite strategically Gawde's time-keeping apparatus provides no markers to quantify time. Through the disorienting movement of twenty-eight moons, our convenient notions of duration get inverted. As the moons change shape at different speeds we are simultaneously confronted with a sense of uncertainty and ennui, the kind of unease that might be quite the inverse of Almond's pounding reminders of passing time. Gawde points out the fact that the differing rotational speeds, the varying dimensions of the twenty-eight moons and their many combinations will ensure that the overall formal configuration of 'Alliteration' cannot look identical for very long periods of time. Enshrined in this constant change is a promise of recreation; however the process continues without beginning or end, without intervals or a possible culmination in sight. Such a paradoxical feeling of stasis is central to the construction of 'Alliteration'.

As a parting thought it might be instructive to recall Nietzsche's proposition of 'eternal recurrence'; the belief that everything that has happened or will happen, has already occurred infinitely and will continue to recur in a self-similar form. With 'Alliteration', Gawde plays the mischievous horologist, employing a simple mechanical device to tease out a larger metaphysical dialogue.

(Mumbai, March 2009)

JITISH KALLAT (born Mumbai, 1974) has held more than 20 solo exhibitions of his work in leading galleries such as Gallery Chemould and Chemould Prescott Road (Mumbai), Haunch of Venison (Zürich and London), Arario Gallery (Beijing and Seoul), Nature Morte (Delhi), among others.

Kallat's work has been shown at museums, foundations and institutions across the world, including Tate Modern (London), Martin-Gropius-Bau (Berlin), the Gallery of Modern Art (Brisbane), Kunstmuseum Berne (Berne), the Serpentine Gallery (London), the Mori Art Museum (Tokyo), Palais de Beaux-Arts (Brussels), Hangar Bicocca (Milan), the Busan Museum of Modern Art, the Astrup Fearnley Museum of Modern Art (Oslo), Zentrum für Kunst und Medientechnologie/ ZKM (Karlsruhe), Henie Onstad Kunstsenter (Oslo), the Arken Museum of Modern Art (Copenhagen), Institut Valencia d'Art Modern (Valencia), the Art Gallery of Ontario (Toronto), the Royal Academy of Art (London), the Art Gallery of New South Wales (Sydney), and the Gemeente Museum (The Hague), among many others. Kallat's work has been exhibited as part of numerous biennales and triennales including the Havana Biennale, the Gwangju Biennale, the Asia Pacific Triennale, the Fukuoka Asian Art Triennale, and the Guangzhou Triennale, among others. He writes frequently on the subject of contemporary art. Jitish Kallat lives and works in Mumbai, India.

Alliteration

2008-09

mobile sculpture

polyurethane-painted mild steel,
motorised mechanism with drive and
controller etc.

229 x 457 x 76 cms

3 + A/P

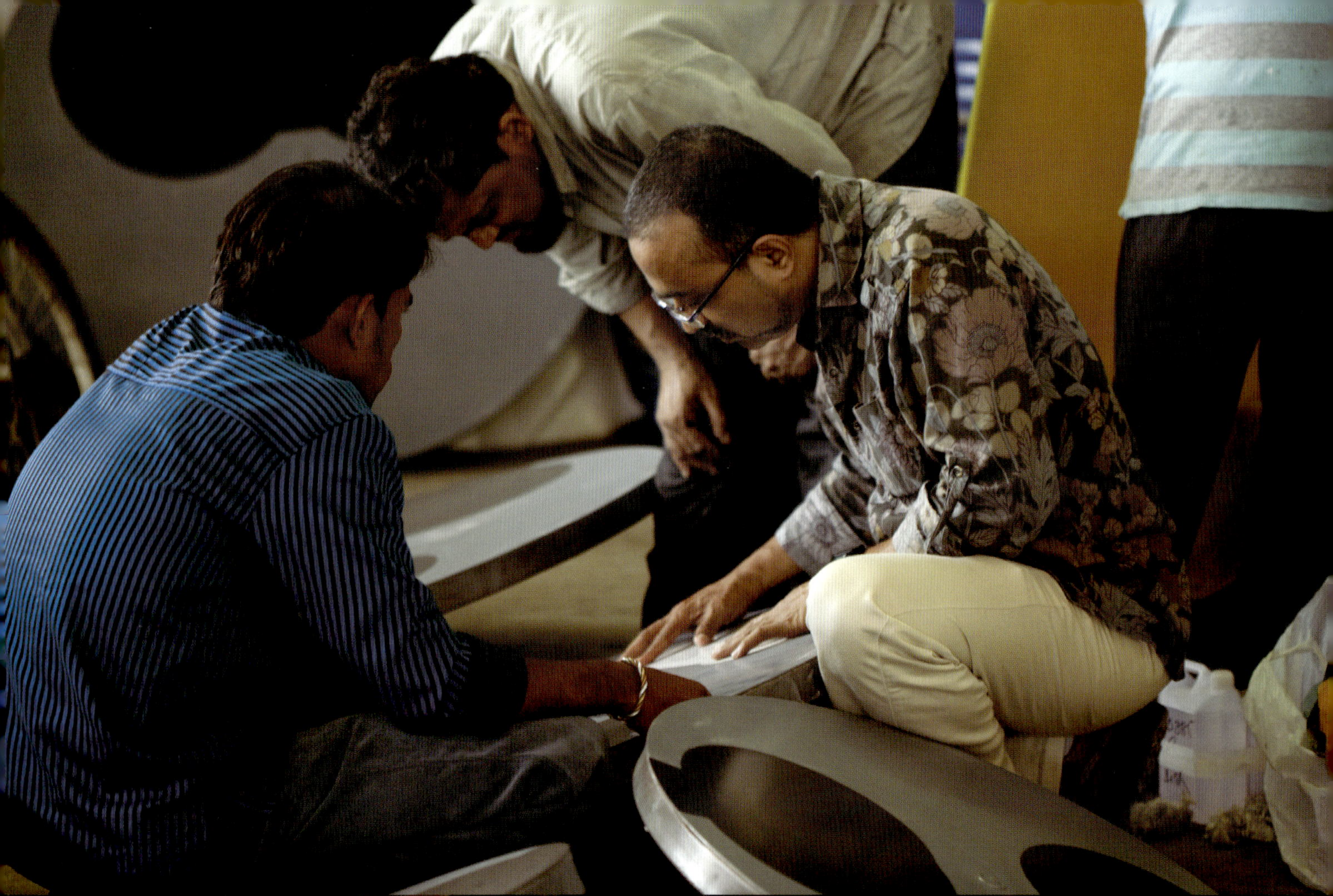

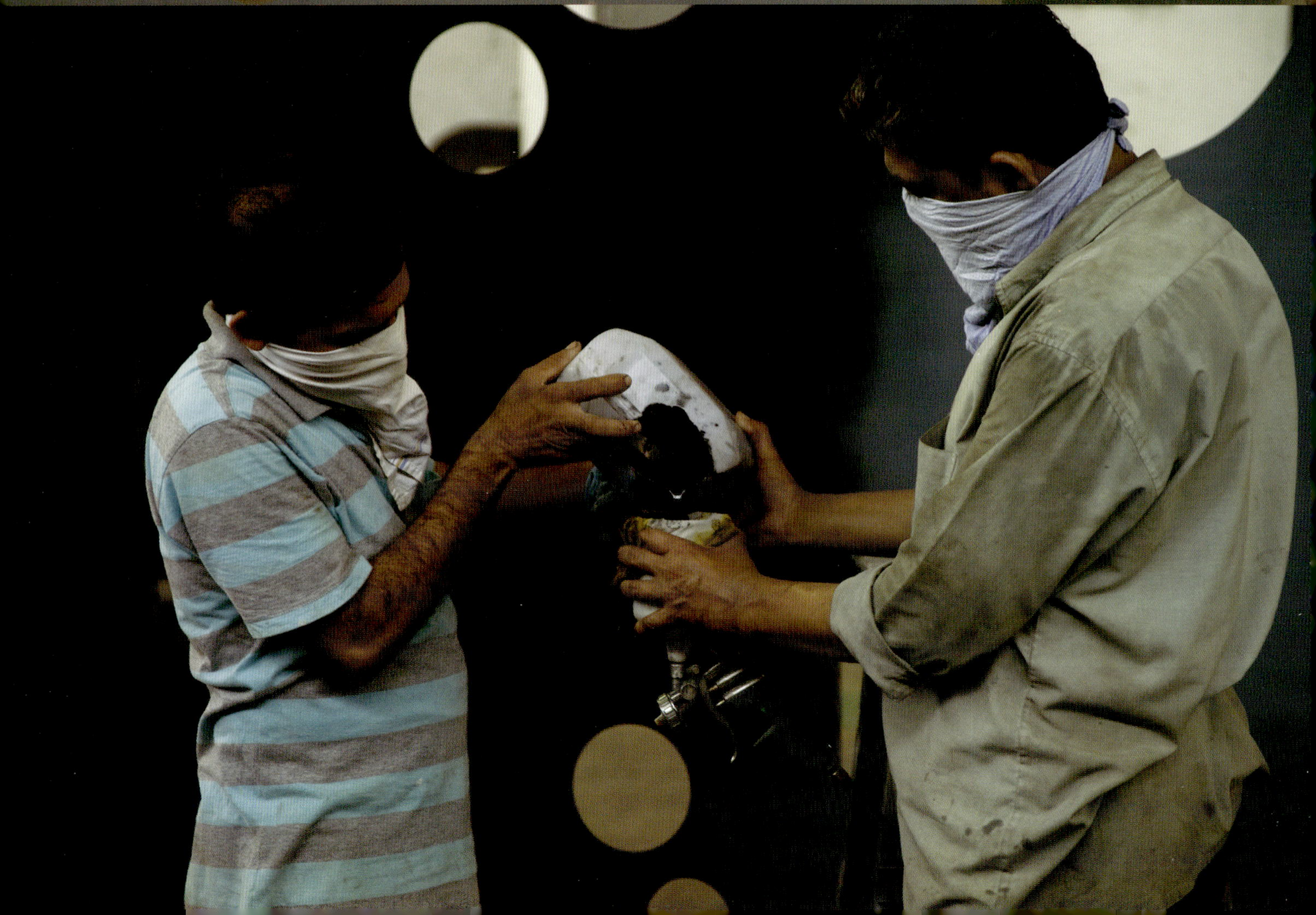

STILL ALIVE - II

2008

sculpture

teakwood, nails,
gas torch etc.

23 x 30 x 33 cms (each) set of 4

3 + 2 A/P

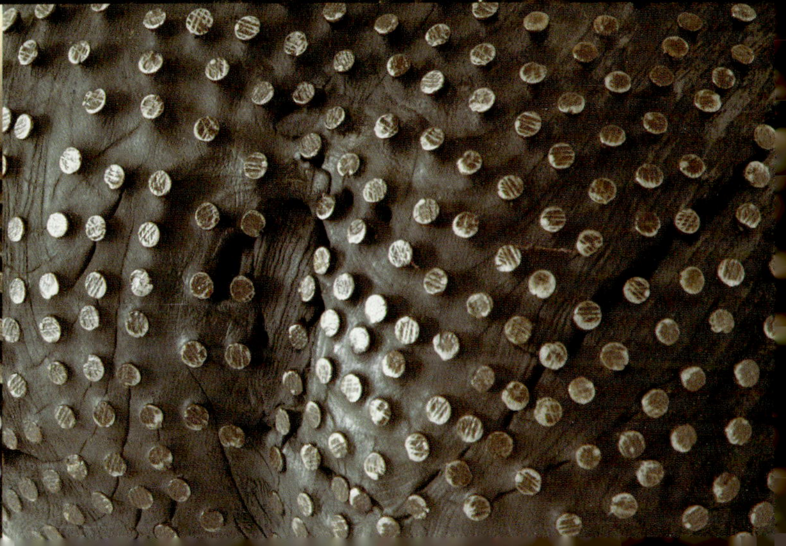

Fly Away – Swim Closer

2008

sculpture

painted fibreglass, inbuilt permanent magnets,
laser printouts, metal wire,
UV tubelights etc.

167 x 90 x 90 cms

3 + A/P

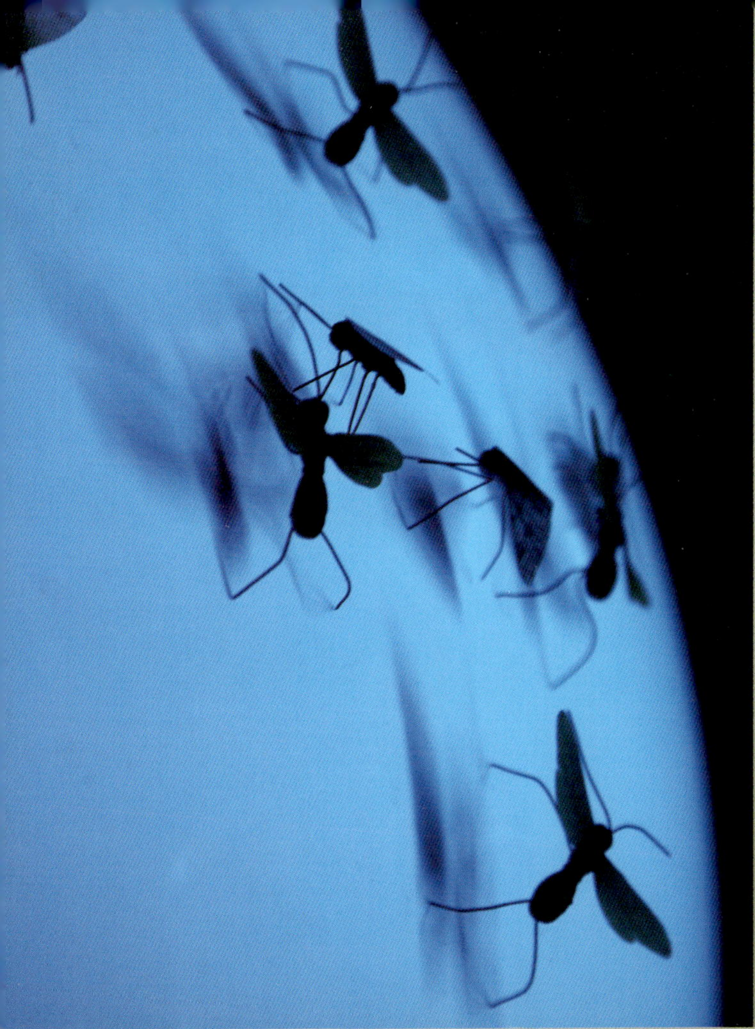

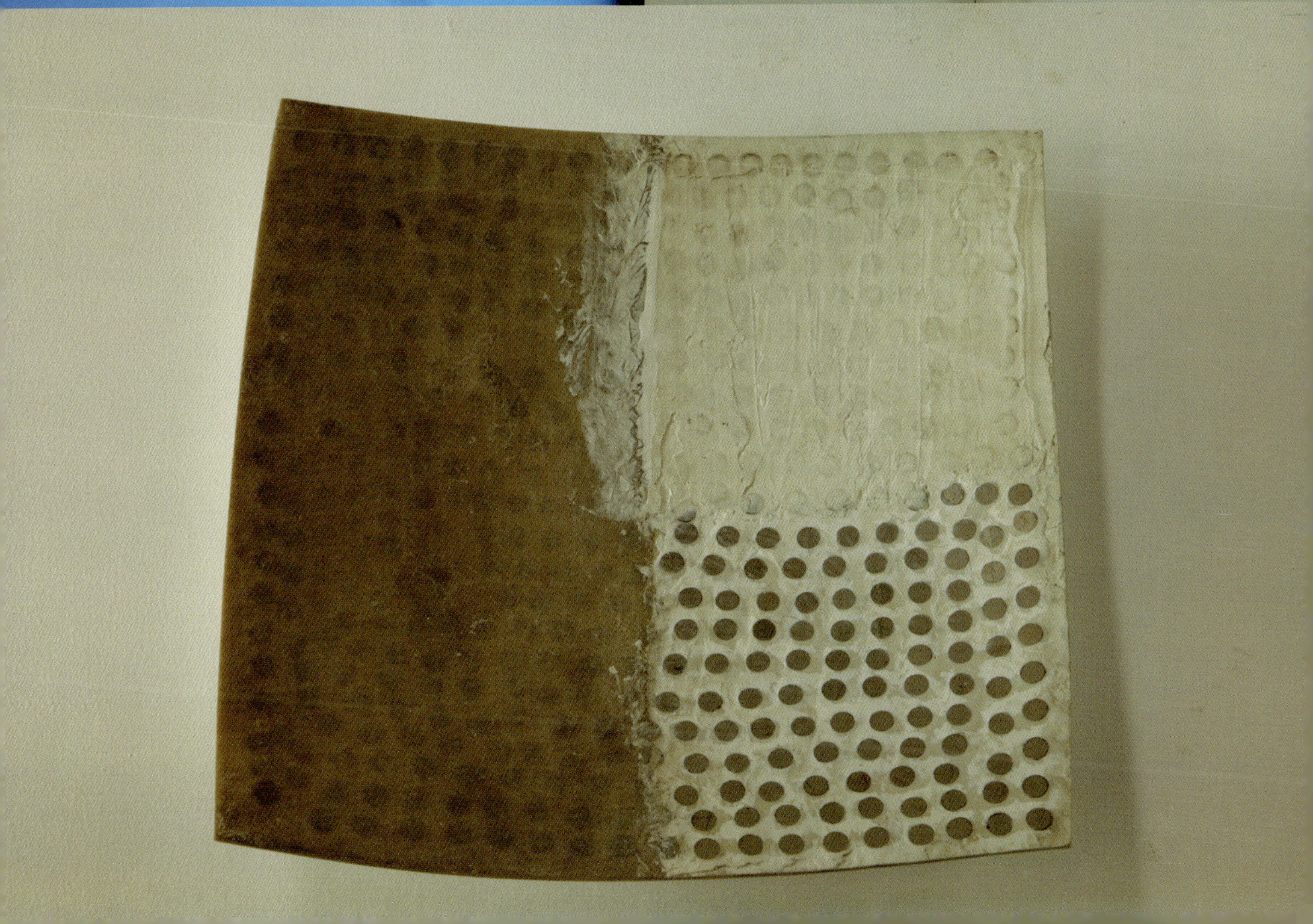

It's All In The Mind

2007

sculpture

translucent resin,
painted fibreglass etc.

23 x 30 x 33 cms (each) set of 6

7 + A/P

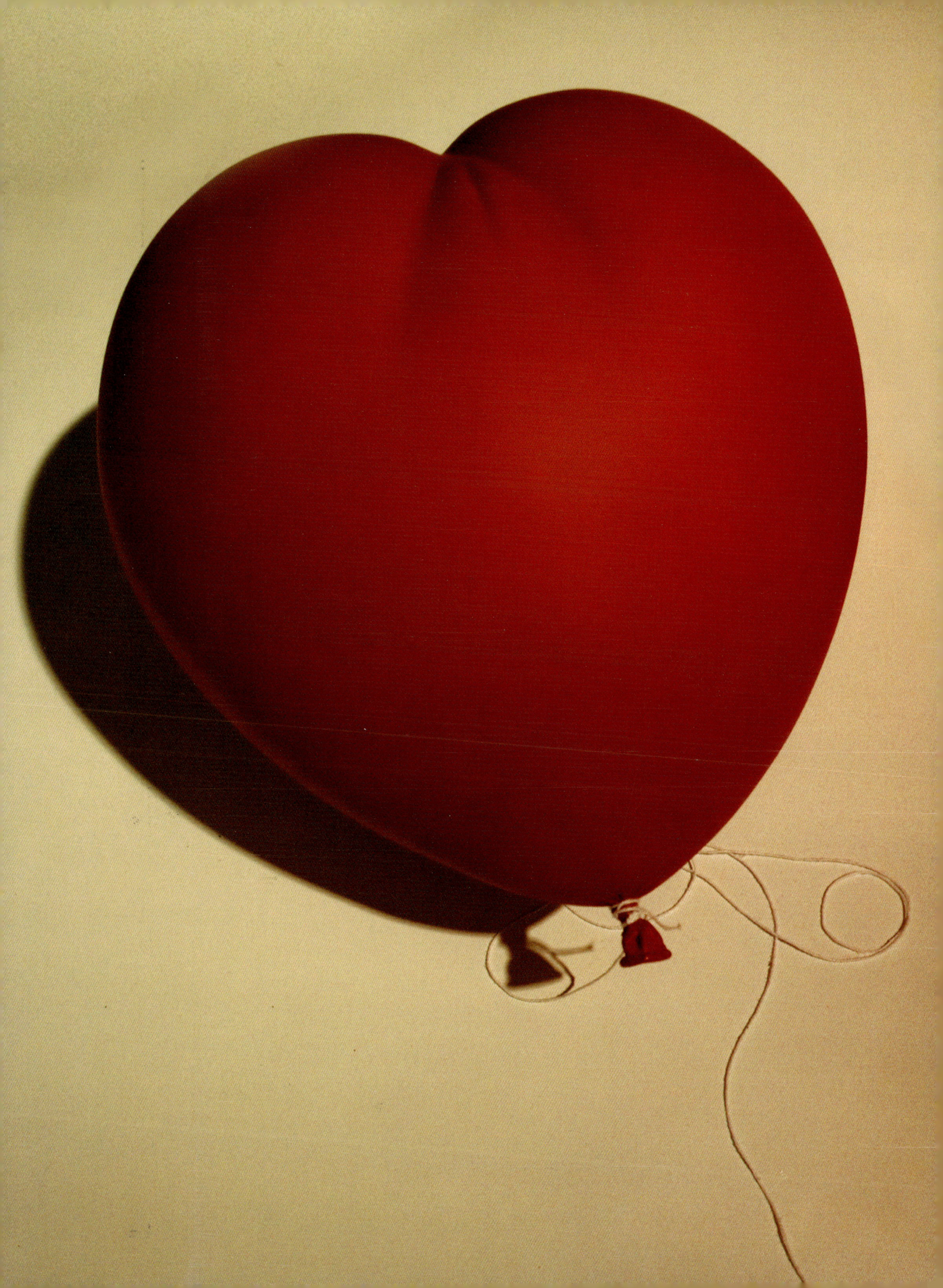

Virtually Untouchable – I

2004-05

mobile sculpture

razor blades, aluminium composite sheet,
super glue, motorised mechanism with drive and controller,
mounted on metal I-beam etc.

333 x 122 x 122 cms

3 + A/P

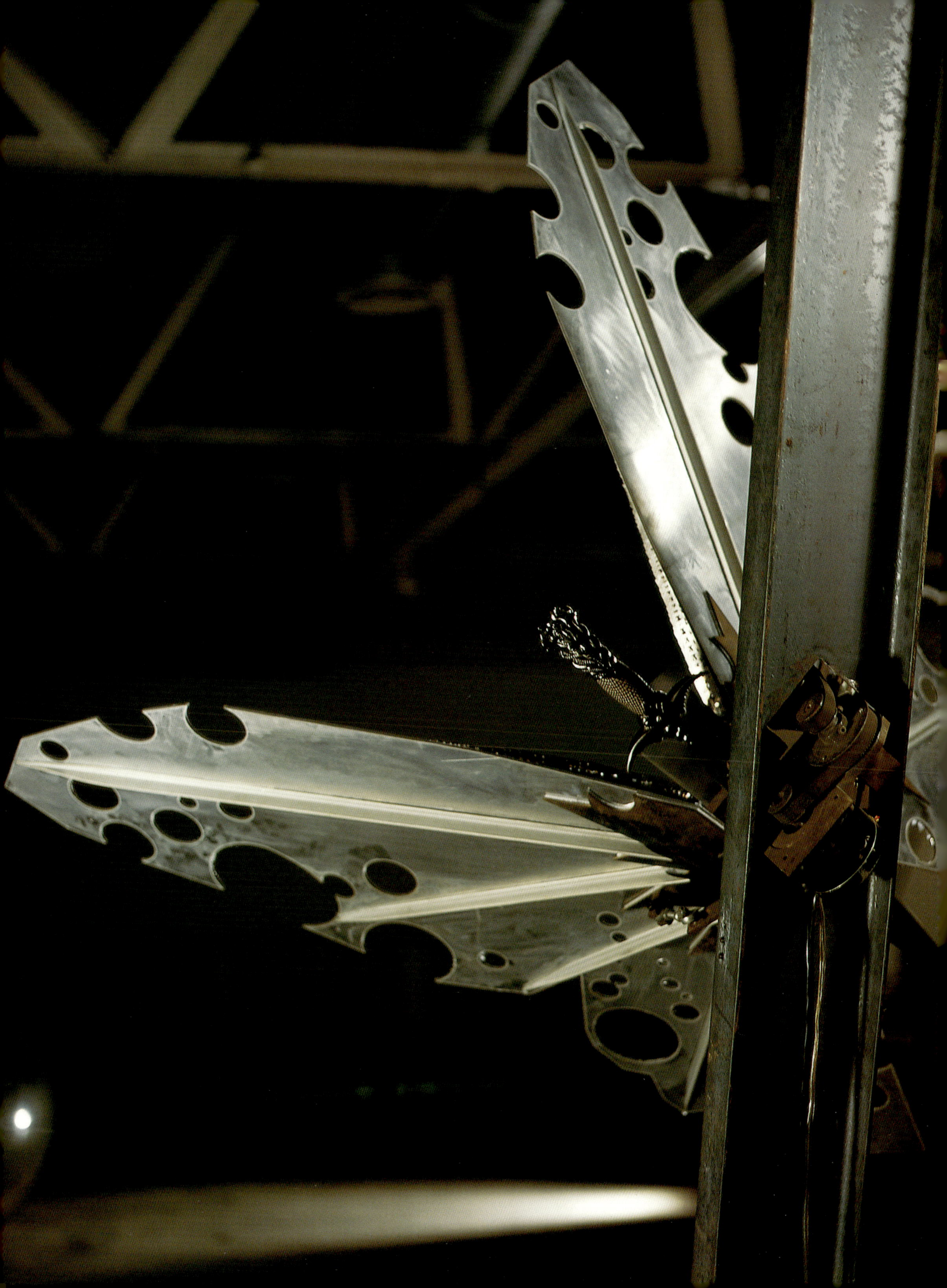

WILKINSON

From the series – Blind Bulb etc...

2004-05

mobile sculpture

mirror-finish stainless steel, painted mild steel,
motorised mechanism with drive etc.

326 x 122 x 90 cms

3 + A/P

Virtually Untouchable - III

2007

sculpture

powder-coated razor blades,
stainless steel wire, readymade decorative roses,
wooden chair etc.

garland-170 x 20 x 11 cms (each) set of 3
wooden chair-90 x 50 x 50 cms

3 + A/P

Blind Bulbs

2006-07

sculpture

polyurethane-painted fibreglass
333 x 181 x 181 cms (each) set of 3

DIECI

DIECI

AMMANN
YANMAR

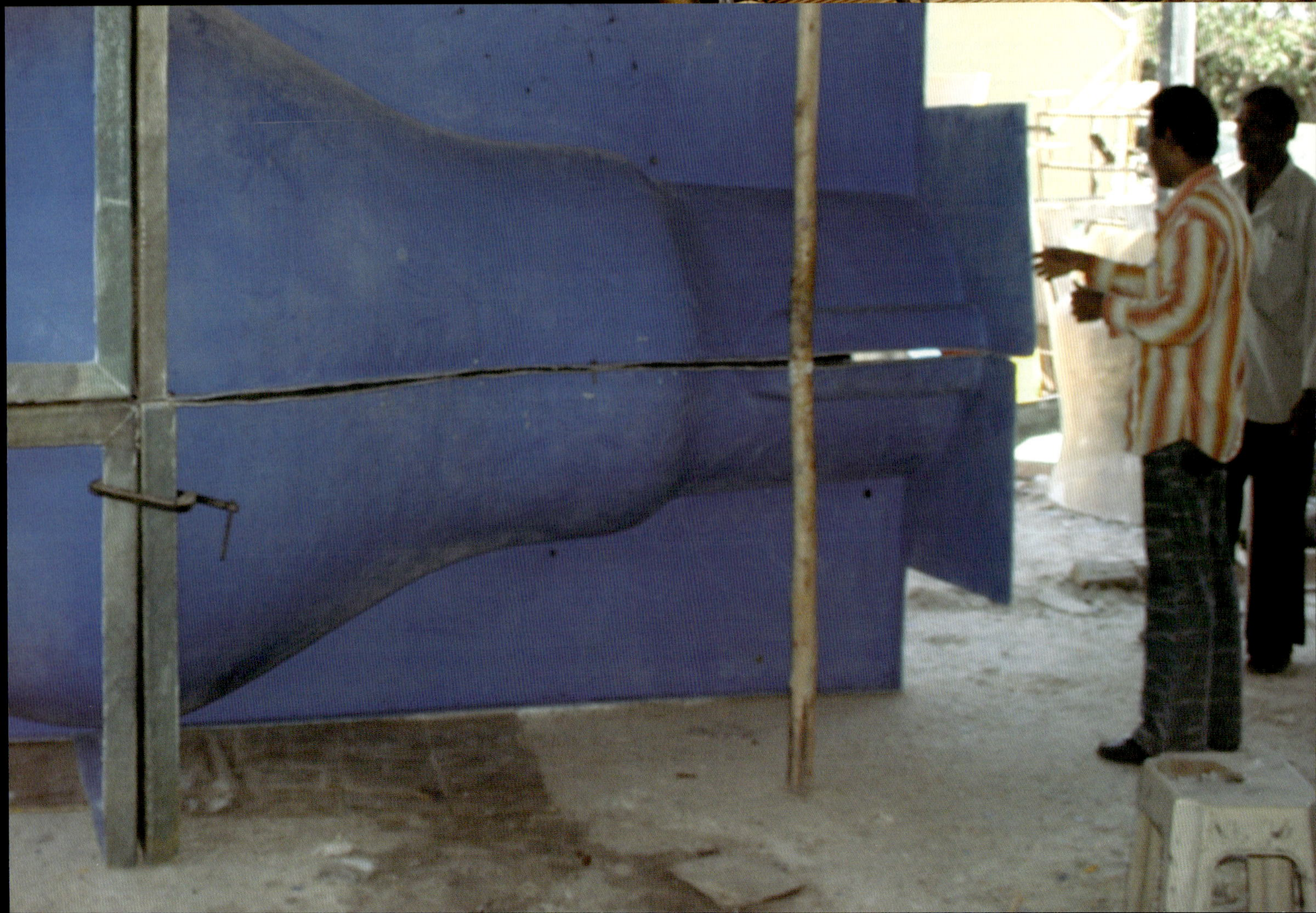

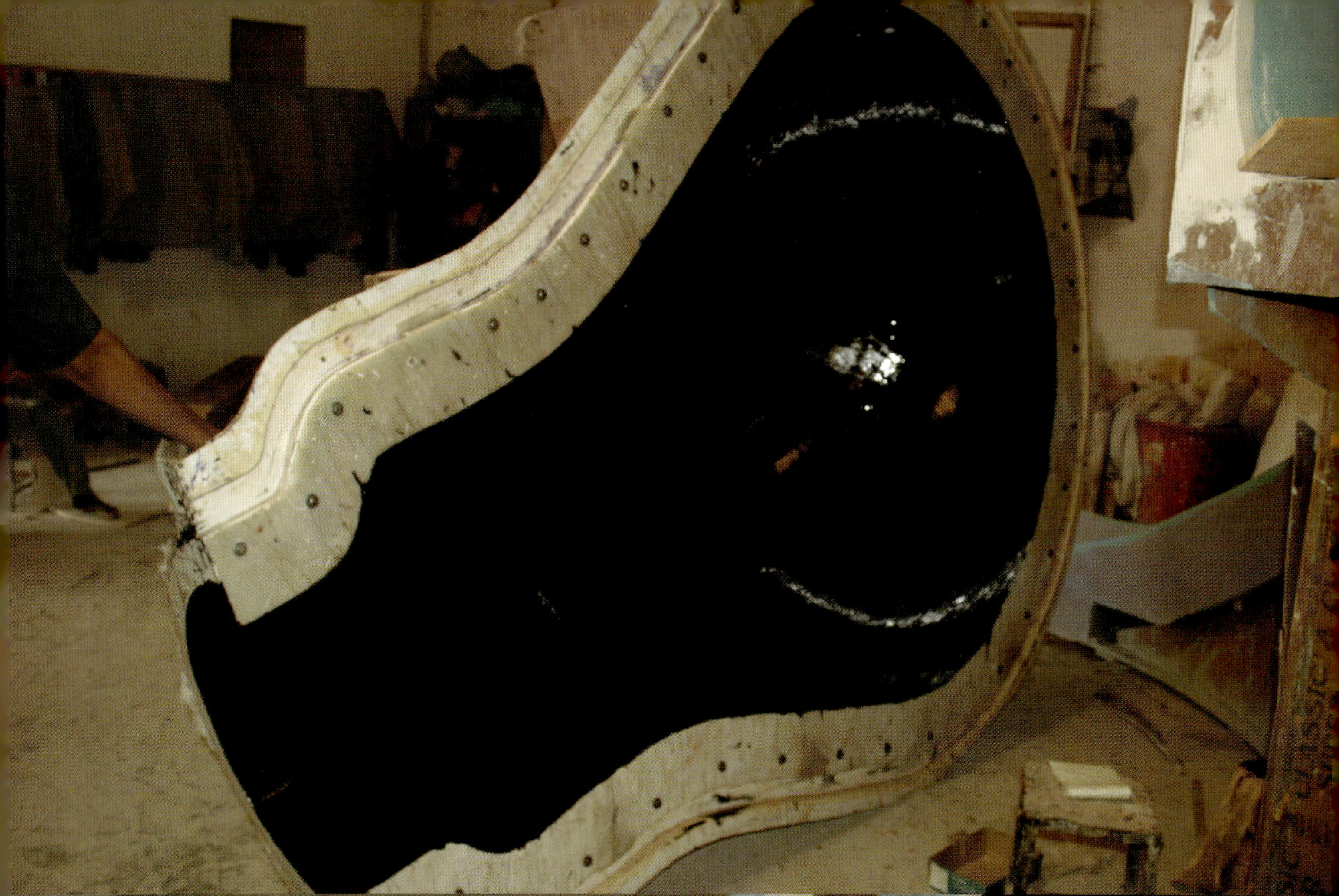

JAR

Life

2006-07

sculpture

bronze cast

83 x 81 x 53 cms

3 + A/P

Ghost in the Bottle

2007

sculpture

mirror-finished glass, wood etc.

size variable

3 + A/P

From the series - Blind Bulb etc...

2004-05

mobile sculpture

foam rubber, acrylic mirror, plywood,
motorised mechanism etc.

167 x 425 x 23 cms

3 + A/P

Virtually Untouchable - II

2005-06

sculpture

razor blades, super glue,
acrylic sheet etc.

6.5 x 106 x 212 cms

Still Alive – I

2006

mobile sculpture

cast resin, painted fibreglass,
motorised mechanism with drive / controller etc.

3 + A/P

Arrival – Departure

2007

sculpture

mirror-finish stainless steel
epoxy-painted mild steel etc.

155 x 335 x 33 cms

3 + A/P

arrival departure

Virtually Untouchable – IV

2006-07

sculpture

mirror-finish stainless steel etc.

size variable

7 + 3 A/P

From the series – Blind Bulb etc...

2004-05

sculpture

cast resin, painted fibreglass,
metal balls etc.

167 x 90 x 90 cms

3 + 1 A/P

Heart Beat – Beat Heart

2009

sculpture

painted fibreglass, nails etc.

size variable, set of 8

7 + A/P

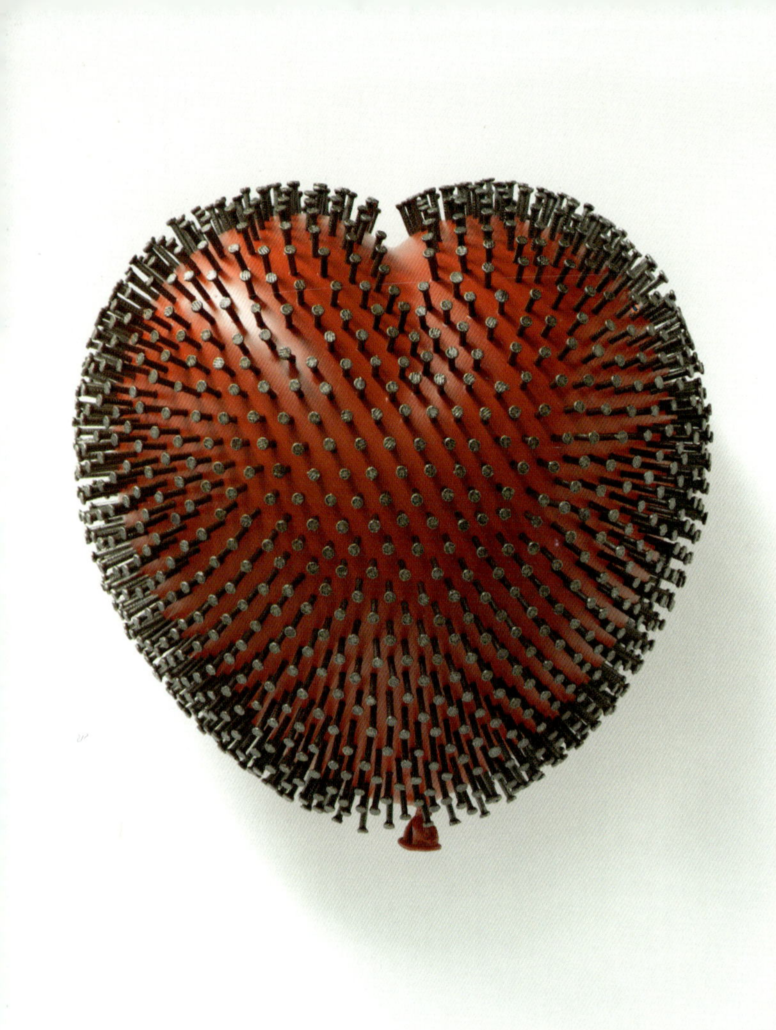
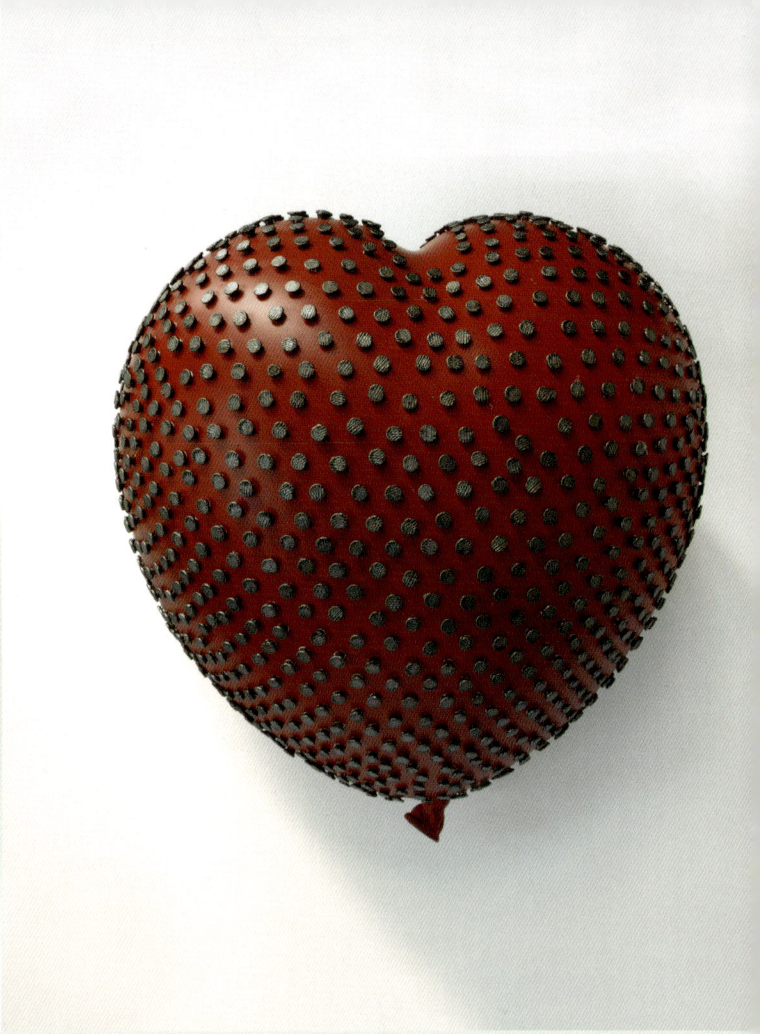
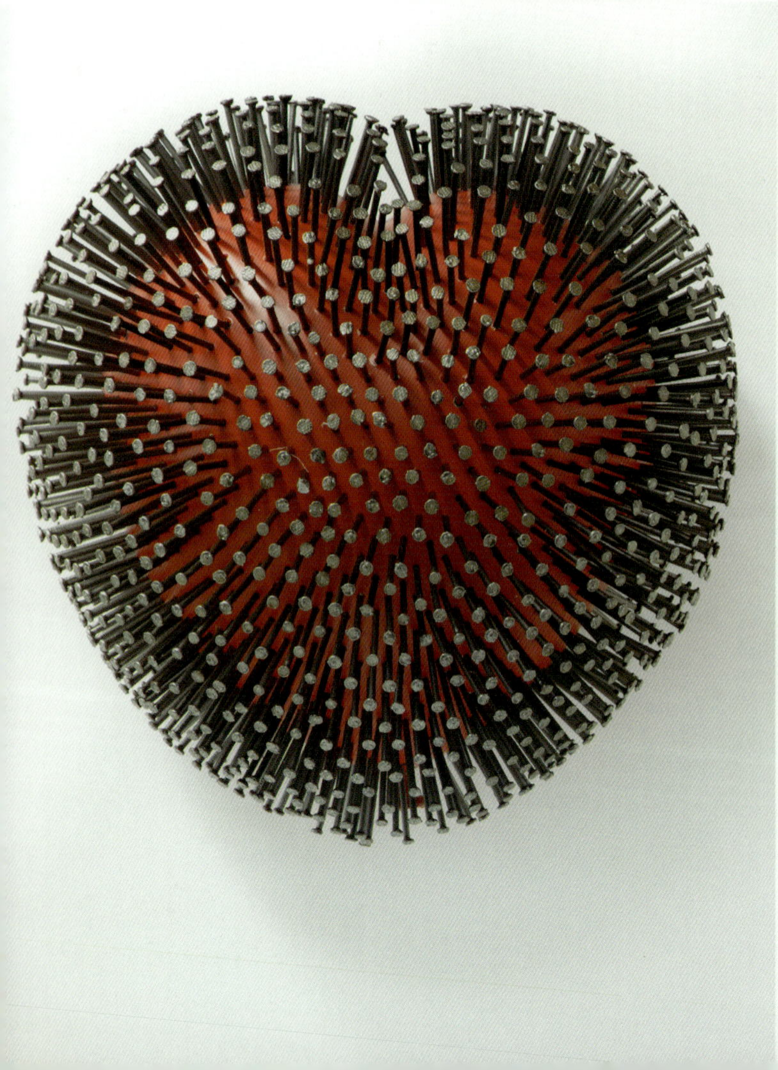
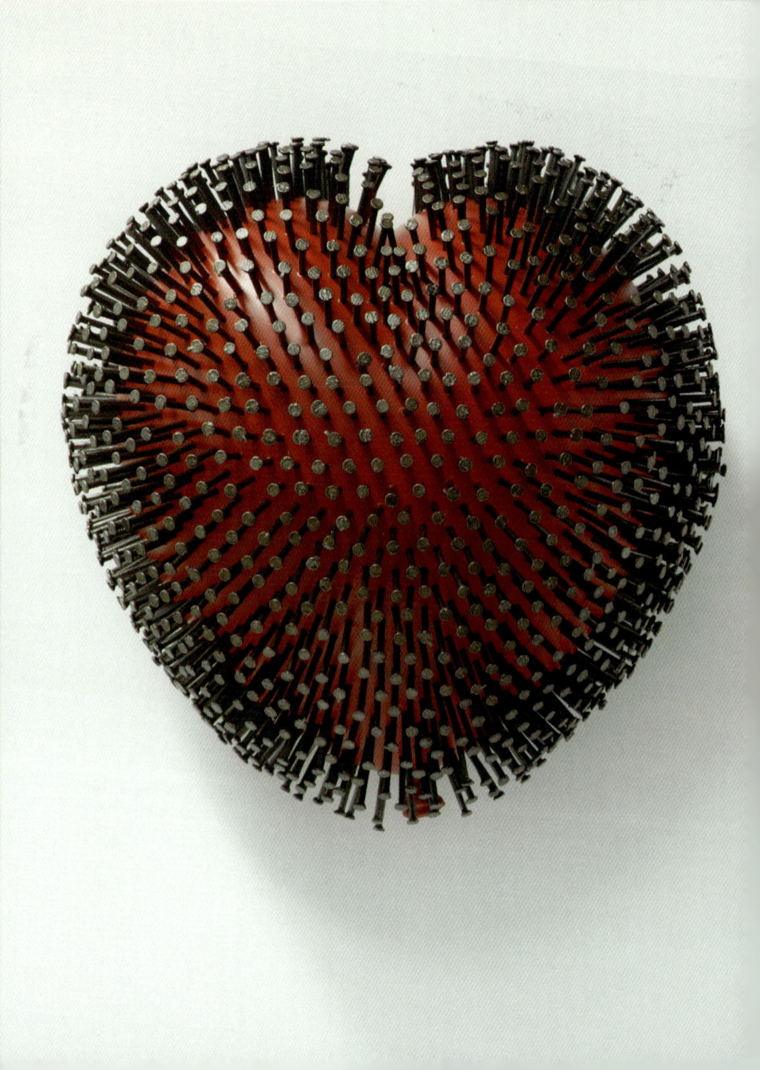

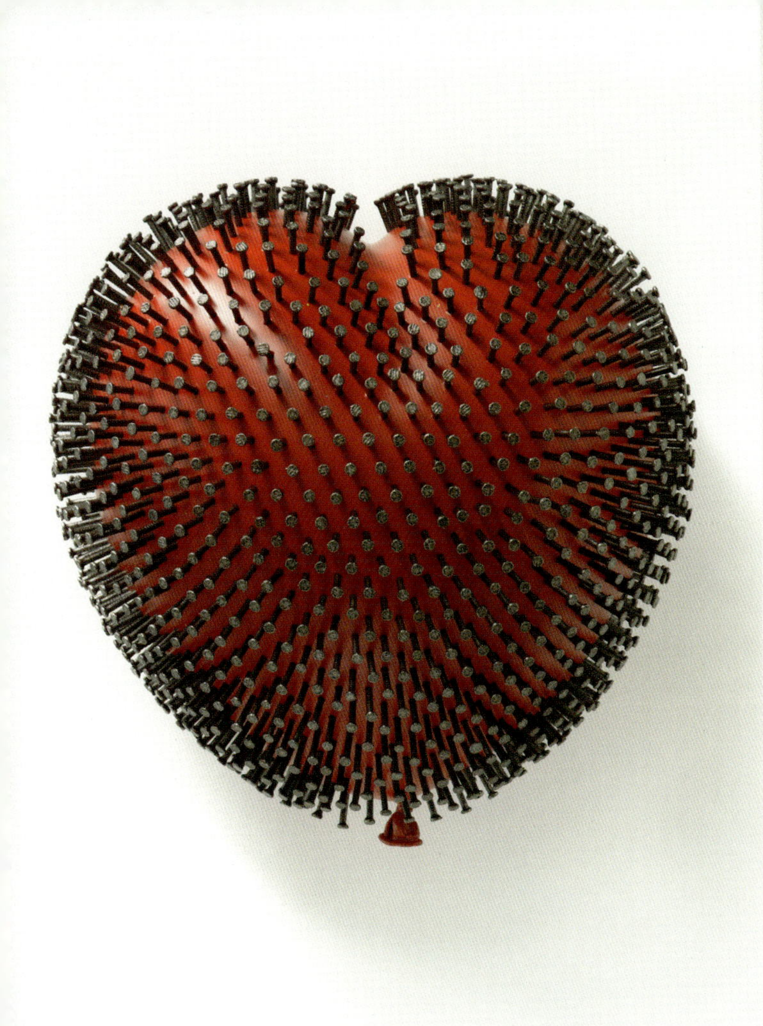

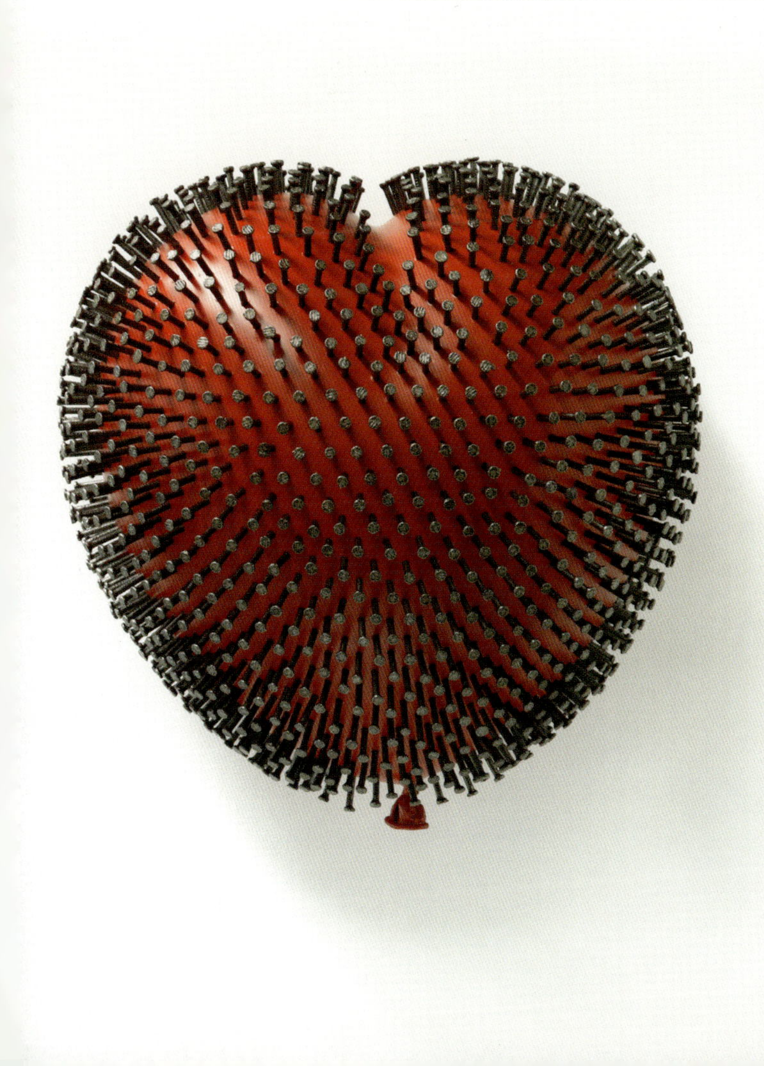

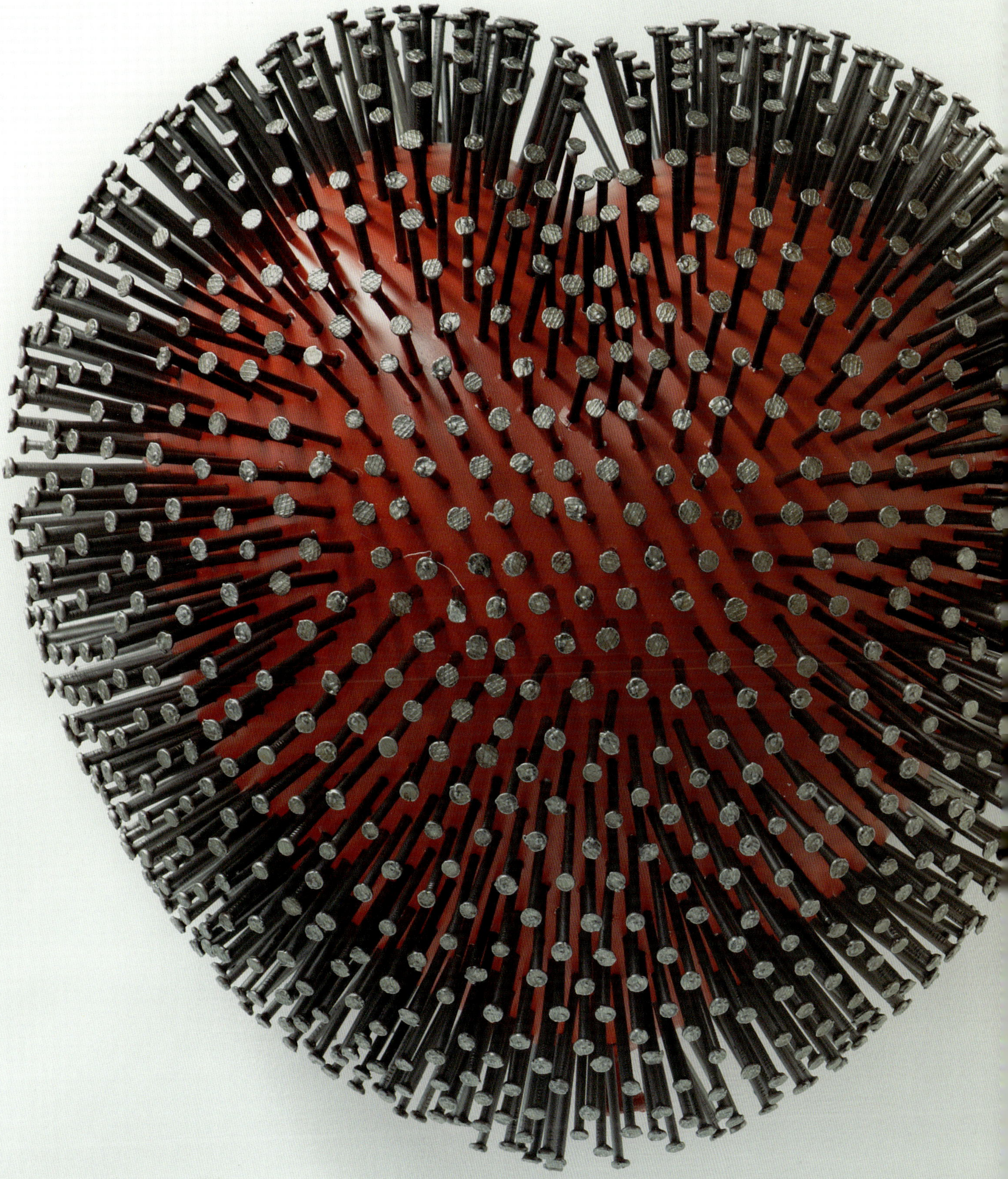

Sunil Gawde was born in Mumbai in 1960. He graduated in fine art from the Sir Jamsetjee Jejeebhoy School of Art, Mumbai, in 1980. In 1995, he received the British Council's Charles Wallace Award for 1995-1996, and spent a year as visiting artist at the Glasgow School of Art, Scotland.

Since 1990, Gawde has held 11 solo exhibitions of his paintings, sculptures, installations and composite works, including 'Radium Grass' (Mackintosh Museum, Glasgow, 1997), '1 mm' (Sakshi Gallery, Mumbai, 2001), '8 seconds ahead of time' (Sakshi Gallery, Bangalore, 2002), 'Blind bulb etc' (Sakshi Gallery, Mumbai and Delhi, 2005).

Gawde's work has also been exhibited in the context of curated exhibitions such as 'Bombay: Maximum City' (Lille, 2006), 'Made by Indians' (St Tropez, 2006), organised by Galerie Enrico Navarra, Paris, and 'Art on the Corniche' (Abu Dhabi, 2007), organised by Galerie Enrico Navarra and the Abu Dhabi Authority for Culture and Heritage. Gawde's work was also exhibited at SHContemporary (Shanghai, 2007), Pulse Miami (Miami, 2008) and ARCO 09 (Madrid, 2009).

Gawde was invited to participate in the 53rd Venice Biennale (2009), curated by Daniel Birnbaum.

Reflecting on the transition he has made in recent years, from a painter's studio practice to the collaborative workshop practice of a sculptor and installation artist, Gawde writes: "To my mind, the marriage of philosophy, technique, aesthetics and material is the foundation of my creative process. An essential element of my sculptures is also the technical skill of the experts that I work with. While canvases are a solitary effort, science-based sculptural creations, which have to be aesthetically perfect and structurally sound, require a skilful combination of engineering and art."

Foundation B&G

Foundation B&G is a visual arts initiative of Popular Prakashan, an 85-year-old publishing house that pioneered high-quality publishing in the social sciences, history and literature in India. The Foundation aims to develop a serious knowledge infrastructure for India's contemporary visual arts. Its mission is to inform the enthusiast and to augment the bandwidth of the informed. The Foundation has planned a publishing programme that includes entry-level, intermediate and specialist books. It proposes to collaborate with artists towards realising ambitious projects. It will work towards achieving a convergence among artists, critics, curators, viewers and readers. At school level, it will model an art pedagogy that is responsive and participatory: to cultivate new generations that will not regard culture as alien to normal life, but will embrace it as a necessary condition of being. Ranjit Hoskote, well-known poet, curator and critic, is Curatorial Advisor and Series Editor, Foundation B&G.

The Foundation's parent organisation, Popular Prakashan, counts among its authors such seminal thinkers as the sociologist G S Ghurye, the historians D D Kosambi and Romila Thapar, and the political thinker Jayaprakash Narayan. Its avant-garde list in Marathi literature includes some of postcolonial India's most distinguished poets, playwrights and fiction writers, including Vijay Tendulkar, V. V. Shirwadkar, Vinda Karandikar and Gangadhar Gadgil. In recent decades, Popular's list has been expanded to include authors like the celebrity chef Sanjeev Kapoor and the legendary actor Amitabh Bachchan. Popular has also carved a reputation for itself in the area of general books and children's books. Popular's association with Encyclopaedia Britannica, Star Television, Discovery Channel and other partners has ensured that its books are widely distributed in India and abroad.